DINOSAUR Academy

Fractions and Decimals

ARCTURUS

Key skills in this book

Understanding fractions..........................4	Understanding tenths and hundredths..........................51
Ordering unit fractions............................14	Converting fractions to decimals......53
Ordering non-unit fractions....................15	Adding fractions and decimals..........59
Counting up in fractions..........................18	Adding units and decimals..................60
Equivalent fractions.................................20	Dividing units by 10................................62
Simplifying fractions................................27	Dividing units by 100..............................63
Ordering equivalent fractions..............28	Rounding..64
Comparing fractions................................29	Ordering decimals....................................66
Adding fractions..30	Comparing decimals 67
Subtracting fractions...............................36	Adding decimals..68
Improper fractions....................................42	Converting decimals to fractions......72
Understanding tenths..............................44	Introducing percentages........................74
Tenths as decimals....................................48	Further practice...80

This edition published in 2023 by Arcturus Publishing Limited
26/27 Bickels Yard, 151–153 Bermondsey Street,
London SE1 3HA

Copyright © Arcturus Holdings Limited

All rights reserved. No part of this publication may be reproduced, stored in a retrieval system, or transmitted, in any form or by any means, electronic, mechanical, photocopying, recording, or otherwise, without prior written permission in accordance with the provisions of the Copyright Act 1956 (as amended). Any person or persons who do any unauthorized act in relation to this publication may be liable to criminal prosecution and civil claims for damages.

Author: Lisa Regan
Illustrator: Claire Stamper
Editors: Donna Gregory and Lucy Doncaster
Designer: Linda Storey
Design Manager: Jessica Holliland
Managing Editor: Joe Harris

ISBN: 978-1-3988-2577-2
CH010835NT
Supplier 29, Date 0523, PI 00003157

Printed in China

Introduction

Welcome to the Dinosaur Academy! Join the dinosaurs and their prehistoric friends as they set out to discover just how much fun fractions and decimals can be.

In this book, you'll find lots of awesome activities that will help you understand fractions and decimals. Start at the beginning, where you will learn about different types of fractions, how to add, subtract, and order them, and how to convert them into decimals. Next, discover how to add, subtract, and order decimals, then how to convert decimals and fractions to percentages. Are you ready? Then grab your pencil, put on your thinking cap, and let's get going!

Whole or half?

This hungry dinosaur has been sorting out some snacks! Write whether each is a whole melon or half a melon.

Of the six snacks, how many are halves?

$\frac{}{6}$

Is that half of them or all of them?

Half of them

All of them

Draw the fraction

These two friends are doing their homework. They need to shade the shapes to show the fractions. Can you help?

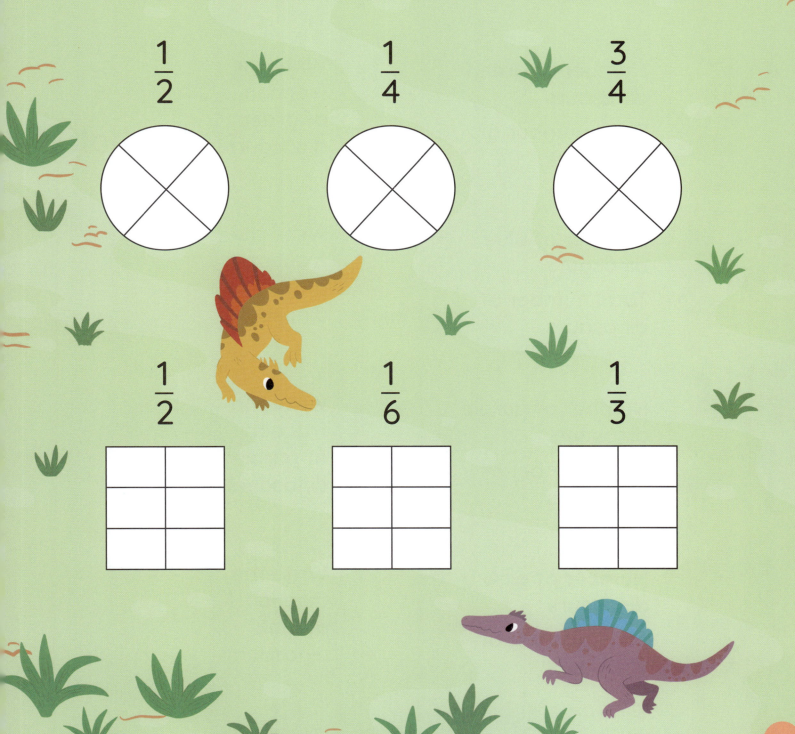

Find the fraction

Study the groups of dinosaurs. Complete the fraction boxes and then write your answers as words. The first one has been done for you.

Number of green dinosaurs [1]
Total number of dinosaurs [2]

Write the fraction of green dinosaurs. $\frac{1}{2}$ half

Number of blue dinosaurs [ ]
Total number of dinosaurs [ ]

Write the fraction of blue dinosaurs.

Number of purple dinosaurs [ ]
Total number of dinosaurs [ ]

Write the fraction of purple dinosaurs.

Number of pink dinosaurs [ ]
Total number of dinosaurs [ ]

Write the fraction of pink dinosaurs.

A fraction with a 1 at the top is called a unit fraction.

How many?

Answer the questions below about the dinosaurs you see here.

Out of the green dinosaurs, how many have spots? ▢/2   Is that half or a third?   half ▢   third ▢

Out of the orange dinosaurs, how many are asleep? ▢/3   Is that half or a third?   half ▢   third ▢

Out of the spotted dinosaurs, how many are standing on two legs? ▢/4   Is that half or a quarter?   half ▢   quarter ▢

Write the fraction

Look at the shapes. Work out how much of each shape is shaded. Find the matching fraction below.

$\frac{1}{2}$ $\frac{1}{3}$ $\frac{1}{4}$ $\frac{1}{5}$ $\frac{1}{6}$

Draw the fraction

These dinosaurs are collecting water. Draw a line to show where the water will come up to each time.

This dinosaur fills the bottle to the one quarter mark. $\frac{1}{4}$

This dinosaur fills the bottle to the halfway mark. $\frac{1}{2}$

This dinosaur fills the bottle to the three quarters mark. $\frac{3}{4}$

Match the fractions

Draw lines to match up the diagrams with the fractions. The first one has been done for you.

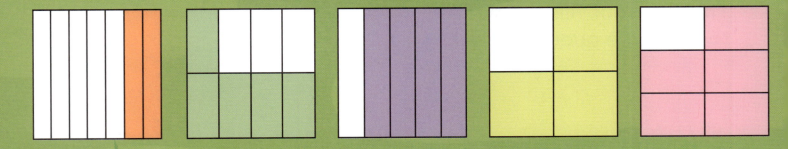

These are all non-unit fractions, which means that the number at the top is greater than 1.

Word problems

Look at the eight dinosaurs here, then answer the questions below.

What fraction have spots?

What fraction have stripes?

What fraction have a green body?

What fraction have plates or spines on their backs?

Picture problems

Can you find the answers to these picture problems?

Circle one fifth of these dinosaurs.

Circle one half of these dinosaurs.

Circle two thirds of these dinosaurs.

Circle five sixths of these dinosaurs.

Circle two fifths of these dinosaurs.

Word problems

Study these 10 dino friends, then answer the questions.
The first one has been done to help you.

What fraction are blue? $\frac{3}{10}$

What fraction have a red head?

What fraction are showing their teeth?

What fraction have a feathered tail?

What fraction are wearing a hat?

What fraction have spotted legs?

Ordering unit fractions

These Lambeosaurus are in a pickle! Can you put the fractions in order on the yellow dots, with the smallest on the left and the largest on the right?

Ordering non-unit fractions

Trace a path from one Pachycephalosaurus to another, starting with the smallest fraction and working up to the largest.

Shade and sort

There are eight spots on each dinosaur. Shade the fraction of spots shown next to each one, then sort them from 1 to 6, where 1 is the least number of spots and 6 is the greatest number.

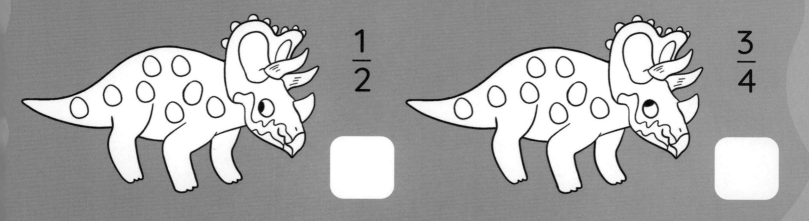

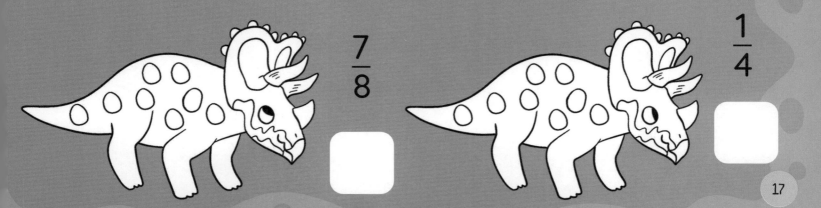

Counting up

Write the ages of these pterosaurs in order in the boxes, from the youngest to the oldest.

What's missing?

These Ankylosaurus are in order, but one is missing.
Draw it in, and write the missing number.

$\frac{1}{4}$ $\frac{1}{2}$ $\frac{3}{4}$ 1

$1\frac{1}{4}$ $1\frac{1}{2}$ 2

Equivalent fractions

Look carefully at these spiders. If half of their legs are dark brown, circle them. If one quarter of their legs are dark brown, count them and write the number in the box below.

Number of spiders with a quarter of their legs in dark brown.

Equivalent fractions

Write the fraction of purple fish next to each pond.
Circle the one that is not equivalent to a third.

Equivalent fractions have the same value, but have different numbers in them.

Fast flyers

Shade the correct number of dragonflies in each group to match the instructions underneath.

Make $\frac{3}{7}$ blue

Make $\frac{4}{7}$ green

Make $\frac{1}{6}$ orange

Make $\frac{5}{6}$ purple

Make $\frac{3}{10}$ purple, $\frac{2}{10}$ green, and the remainder blue.

How many are blue?

Half ☐   A third ☐

Equivalent fractions

Which mighty T. rex does not have a fraction equivalent to a half?

Clock fractions

One hour is 60 minutes, or 12 sets of 5 minutes. Shade these clock faces to see if these facts are true or false. We've done the first one for you.

Equivalent fractions

Learn about equivalent fractions by matching up each dinosaur's circle to one of the fossil fractions.

Equivalent fractions

Moving across, up, and down (but not diagonally), find a way through the grid landing only on fractions that are equivalent to $\frac{1}{2}$.

START

$\frac{1}{2}$	$\frac{2}{4}$	$\frac{6}{12}$	$\frac{1}{7}$	$\frac{2}{5}$	$\frac{3}{4}$
$\frac{1}{8}$	$\frac{1}{4}$	$\frac{12}{24}$	$\frac{2}{3}$	$\frac{3}{5}$	$\frac{8}{10}$
$\frac{3}{9}$	$\frac{2}{9}$	$\frac{4}{8}$	$\frac{11}{13}$	$\frac{8}{9}$	$\frac{5}{7}$
$\frac{4}{6}$	$\frac{6}{12}$	$\frac{9}{18}$	$\frac{1}{5}$	$\frac{3}{8}$	$\frac{7}{9}$
$\frac{10}{14}$	$\frac{5}{10}$	$\frac{1}{10}$	$\frac{3}{10}$	$\frac{4}{9}$	$\frac{4}{5}$
$\frac{1}{9}$	$\frac{11}{22}$	$\frac{10}{20}$	$\frac{8}{16}$	$\frac{3}{6}$	$\frac{1}{2}$

FINISH

Simplifying fractions

Simplify the fractions on these swimming reptiles to complete each row of three.

$\frac{6}{18}$ → $\frac{3}{9}$ → $\frac{1}{\Box}$

$\frac{4}{16}$ → $\frac{2}{8}$ → $\frac{1}{\Box}$

$\frac{4}{20}$ → $\frac{2}{10}$ → $\frac{1}{\Box}$

In order

The numbers on the leaves are mixed up. Write the numbers on each group of leaves into the tower to the right of the group in the correct order, with the smallest at the bottom.

Bigger, smaller, or the same?

Decide whether the fractions on the left are bigger, smaller, or the same as the ones on the right.
Then draw the correct symbol in the box.

> **>** bigger than   **<** smaller than   **=** the same

$\frac{1}{2}$ ☐ $\frac{6}{12}$

$\frac{1}{2}$ ☐ $\frac{7}{12}$

$\frac{3}{12}$ ☐ $\frac{1}{6}$

$\frac{3}{4}$ ☐ $\frac{7}{8}$

$\frac{1}{4}$ ☐ $\frac{5}{16}$

$\frac{4}{8}$ ☐ $\frac{8}{16}$

Adding fractions

Use these shapes to help you learn how to add fractions, like the first example, which has been done for you.

If the denominators are the same, add the numerators.

$$\frac{3}{4} + \frac{1}{4} = \frac{4}{4}$$ or 1 whole

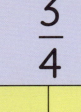

$$\frac{1}{3} + \frac{2}{3} =$$ or 1 whole

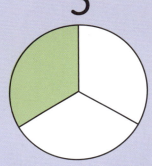 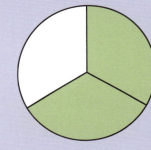

$$\frac{2}{5} + \frac{2}{5} =$$

Adding fractions

Use what you have learned to complete these fraction additions.

$\frac{5}{7} + \frac{1}{7} = \frac{}{}$ $\frac{1}{4} + \frac{2}{4} = \frac{}{}$

$\frac{3}{8} + \frac{3}{8} = \frac{}{}$ $\frac{2}{6} + \frac{3}{6} = \frac{}{}$

$\frac{1}{5} + \frac{3}{5} = \frac{}{}$ $\frac{4}{5} + \frac{1}{5} = \frac{}{}$

$\frac{7}{9} + \frac{1}{9} = \frac{}{}$ $\frac{3}{10} + \frac{6}{10} = \frac{}{}$

Which calculation adds up to 1, or 1 whole? Write it here.

$\frac{}{} + \frac{}{} = \frac{}{}$

Word problems

Answer these word problems by writing the fractions in the boxes.

Half of the creatures are hungry. What fraction are not hungry?

Two fifths of the creatures are male. What fraction are female?

One third of their eggs have hatched. What fraction are unhatched?

If one sixth of them are sauropods and three sixths are flying reptiles, what fraction are neither?

Adding fractions

Read the instructions and fill in the calculations.

Two sixths of these Brachiosaurus have spots.
Draw spots on the plain one to the right.
How many are spotted now?

$$\frac{2}{6} + \frac{1}{6} = \frac{\square}{\square}$$

Now there are equal numbers of spotted and striped dinosaurs. How many in total?

$$\frac{3}{6} + \frac{3}{6} = \frac{\square}{\square}$$

☐ full set of dinosaurs

Adding fractions

Herrerasaurus must choose the fraction with the same denominator to make adding them easy. Circle the cards he should choose and fill in the answers.

$\frac{2}{5} + \boxed{\frac{1}{5}} = \frac{}{}$

$\frac{1}{10} + \boxed{\frac{2}{10}} = \frac{}{}$

$\frac{7}{15} + \boxed{\frac{3}{15}} = \frac{}{}$

More adding

This time, convert the yellow fractions into equivalent fractions so you can work out the answers.

$\dfrac{1}{6} + \dfrac{2}{3} \to \dfrac{}{6} = \dfrac{}{}$ (×2)

$\dfrac{3}{7} + \dfrac{2}{14} \to \dfrac{}{} = \dfrac{}{}$ (÷2)

$\dfrac{5}{8} + \dfrac{3}{4} \to \dfrac{}{} = \dfrac{}{} = \dfrac{}{}$ (×2)

Subtracting fractions

Learn how to subtract fractions with Terry the Triceratops, following the example.

$$\frac{5}{5} - \frac{3}{5} = \frac{2}{5}$$

or 1 whole

$$\frac{2}{3} - \frac{1}{3} = \boxed{}$$

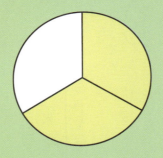 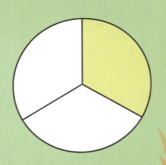 

$$\frac{3}{4} - \frac{1}{4} = \boxed{}$$ or a half

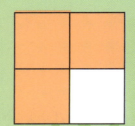 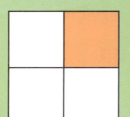 

Subtracting fractions

Terry is keen to learn. Keep trying with him!

$\frac{5}{6} - \frac{1}{6} =$ ☐ $\frac{4}{5} - \frac{1}{5} =$ ☐

$\frac{5}{9} - \frac{2}{9} =$ ☐ $\frac{3}{4} - \frac{2}{4} =$ ☐

$\frac{3}{5} - \frac{2}{5} =$ ☐ $\frac{7}{8} - \frac{5}{8} =$ ☐

$\frac{6}{10} - \frac{3}{10} =$ ☐ $\frac{7}{7} - \frac{6}{7} =$ ☐

The last calculation is the same as subtracting from one whole. Try it again here.

$1 - \frac{6}{7} =$ ☐

Word problems

Answer these word problems by writing the fractions in the boxes.

If two thirds of the fish escape, what fraction are left?

If one quarter of the fish escape, what fraction are left?

If three eighths of the fish get gobbled up, what fraction are left?

If one third of the fish escape, and one third get gobbled up, what fraction are left?

Subtracting fractions

These Euoplocephalus are hungry! If they eat four tenths of the sandwiches, how many are left?

$$1 - \frac{4}{10} = \frac{}{}$$

plate of sandwiches — eaten

If they eat four tenths again tomorrow, how many will be left?

$$\frac{6}{10} - \frac{4}{10} = \frac{}{}$$

Subtracting fractions

Can you help the Herrerasaurus with their subtractions? Convert the pink fractions into equivalent fractions to help you solve these subtraction problems.

$$\frac{6}{7} - \frac{6}{14} \xrightarrow{\div 2} \frac{3}{7} = \frac{3}{7}$$

$$\frac{2}{3} - \frac{3}{9} \xrightarrow{\div 3} \frac{1}{3} = \frac{1}{3}$$

$$\frac{7}{9} - \frac{4}{18} \xrightarrow{\div 2} \frac{2}{9} = \frac{5}{9}$$

Convert the fractions

Convert the calculations below into equivalent fractions with the same denominators, and then solve them. Follow the example, and always choose the smallest denominator possible.

$\dfrac{3}{5} + \dfrac{3}{15} = \dfrac{3}{5} + \dfrac{1}{5} = \dfrac{4}{5}$

$\dfrac{1}{8} + \dfrac{3}{16} = \underline{} + \underline{} = \underline{}$

$\dfrac{33}{100} + \dfrac{3}{10} = \underline{} + \underline{} = \underline{}$

$\dfrac{4}{5} - \dfrac{4}{15} = \underline{} - \underline{} = \underline{}$

$\dfrac{5}{6} - \dfrac{3}{12} = \underline{} - \underline{} = \underline{}$

$\dfrac{12}{25} - \dfrac{12}{50} = \underline{} - \underline{} = \underline{}$

Improper fractions

The dinosaurs have three melons. The melons are cut into eighths. How many eighths are there altogether?

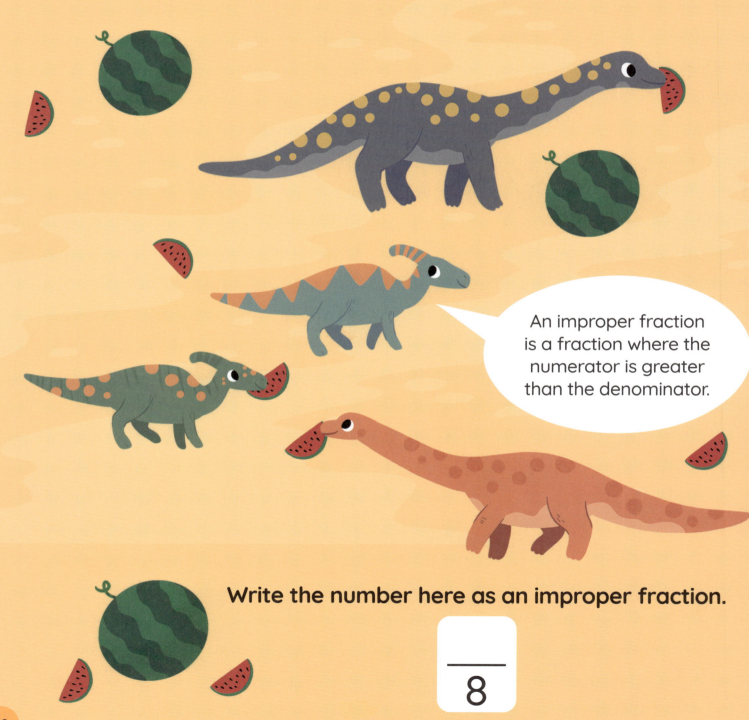

An improper fraction is a fraction where the numerator is greater than the denominator.

Write the number here as an improper fraction.

$\frac{}{8}$

Improper fractions

Here are some more watermelon problems to solve. Remember to count carefully.

Circle the improper fraction and mixed number that these watermelons represent.

  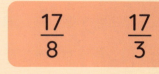

$\frac{17}{8}$ $\frac{17}{3}$

$2\frac{1}{8}$ $2\frac{1}{4}$

Circle the improper fraction and mixed number that these watermelons represent.

$\frac{17}{4}$ $\frac{9}{4}$

$2\frac{1}{4}$ $2\frac{1}{8}$

Circle the improper fraction and mixed number that these watermelons represent.

$\frac{17}{10}$ $\frac{27}{10}$

$2\frac{7}{8}$ $2\frac{7}{10}$

Understanding tenths

These T. rex are trying to get to grips with tenths. See if you can help. Which shape doesn't show one tenth?

Counting in tenths

Count in tenths using these number lines. How many tenths have the pterosaurs flown? Write it in numbers and words.

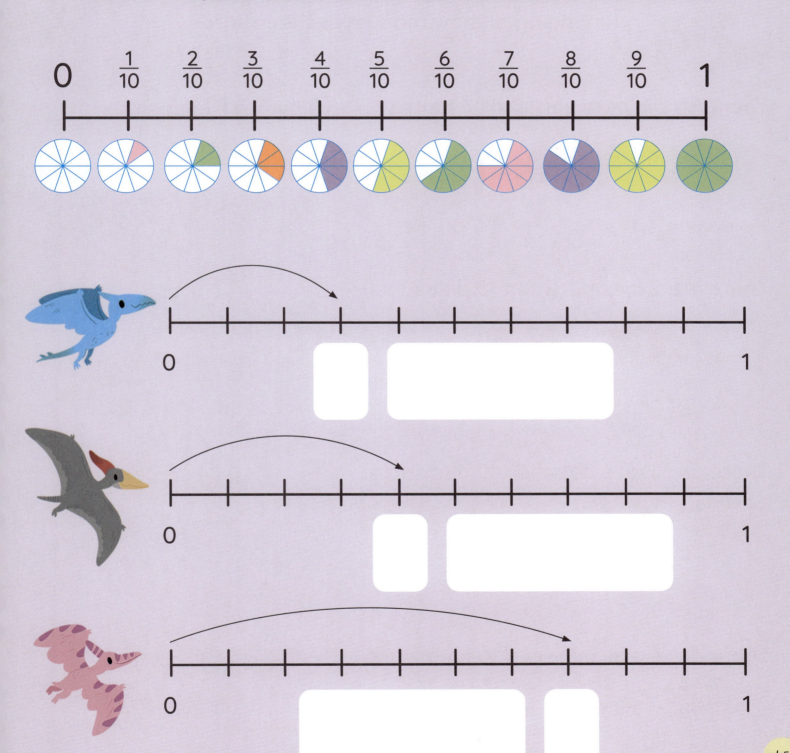

What's a tenth?

Ten dinosaur friends have formed a pie club. Work out how much each dinosaur gets, depending on how many pies they share.

There is 1 pie between 10 dinosaurs.	1 ÷ 10 =

There are 2 pies between 10 dinosaurs.	2 ÷ 10 =

There are 5 pies between 10 dinosaurs.	5 ÷ 10 =

There are 6 pies between 10 dinosaurs.	6 ÷ 10 =

What's a tenth?

Use your knowledge of equivalent fractions to work out these problems.

There are 5 cherry buns to share between 10 dinosaurs. What fraction does each dinosaur get?

$\frac{1}{10}$ of 5 =

There are 15 cherry buns to share between 10 dinosaurs. What fraction does each dinosaur get?

$\frac{15}{10}$ of 10 =

There are 10 cherry buns to share between 10 dinosaurs. What fraction does each dinosaur get?

$\frac{10}{10}$ of 10 =

Writing tenths as decimals

Fill in the missing fractions and their equivalent decimals on the number line, then shade in the correct number of squares on each column below.

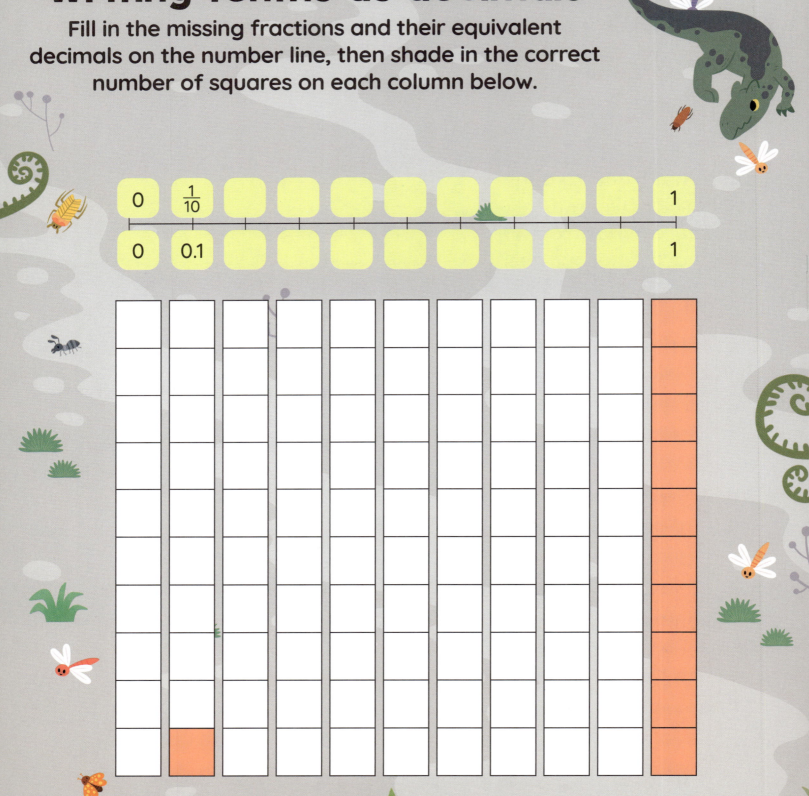

Odd one out

Which rock is the odd one out?
Help the crested dinosaurs decide.

two tenths

0.2

$\frac{2}{10}$

$2\frac{1}{10}$

Ordering decimals

Who's hiding here? Connect the dots in order from 0 to 2.7 to find out.

Tenths and hundredths

The top grid shows tenths. The bottom grid shows hundredths. Can you answer the questions below?

Three tenths are dark pink. How many tenths are light pink?

Count the remaining tenths and fill in the calculations.

$\frac{3}{10} + \frac{5}{10} + \underline{} = 1$

$0.3 + 0.5 + \square = 1$

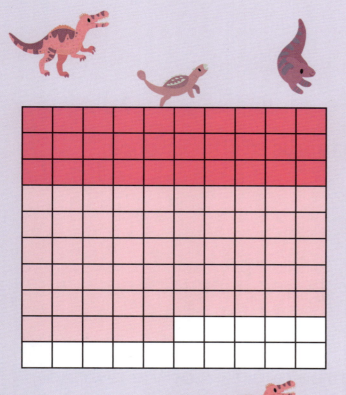

Thirty hundredths are dark pink. How many hundredths are light pink?

Count the remaining hundredths and fill in the calculations.

$\frac{30}{100} + \frac{55}{100} + \underline{} = 1$

$0.3 + 0.55 + \square = 1$

On the move

Each of these friendly flyers can cover different distances. Draw in the distance for the second and third ones.

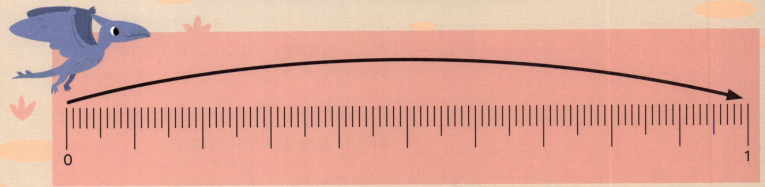

Number one flies this distance.

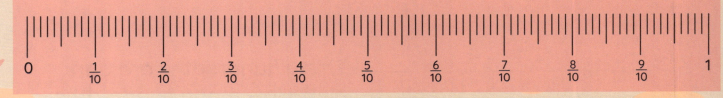

Number two flies six tenths of the distance.

Number three flies three quarters of the distance.

Place value

Can you solve these place value questions? Convert the fractions into decimals and fill in the grids. The first one has been done for you.

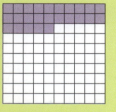 $\frac{25}{100}$ =

units		tenths	hundredths
0	.	2	5

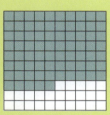 $\frac{75}{100}$ =

units		tenths	hundredths
0	.		

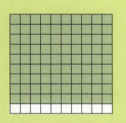 $\frac{9}{10}$ =

units		tenths	hundredths
0	.		

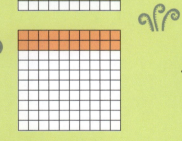 $\frac{2}{10}$ =

units		tenths	hundredths
0	.		

 $\frac{11}{100}$ =

units		tenths	hundredths
0	.		

 $\frac{45}{100}$ =

units		tenths	hundredths
0	.		

Fractions to decimals

Follow the example below to complete these decimal tables.

  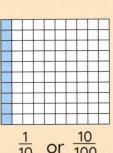 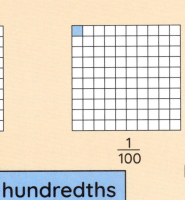

1 whole $\frac{1}{10}$ or $\frac{10}{100}$ $\frac{1}{100}$

units		tenths	hundredths
1	.	1	1

Fraction

$1\frac{11}{100}$

Equivalent decimal

1.11

 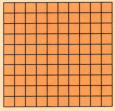 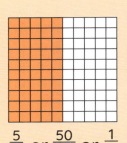  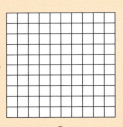

1 whole $\frac{5}{10}$ or $\frac{50}{100}$ or $\frac{1}{2}$ 0

units		tenths	hundredths
	.		

Fraction

$1\frac{1}{2}$

Equivalent decimal

 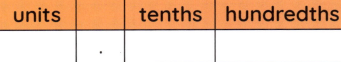

0     $\frac{3}{10}$ or $\frac{30}{100}$ $\frac{5}{100}$

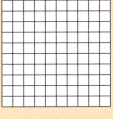 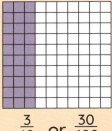 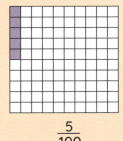 

units		tenths	hundredths
	.		

Fraction

$\frac{35}{100}$

Equivalent decimal

Fractions to decimals

Complete these decimal tables, following the previous examples.

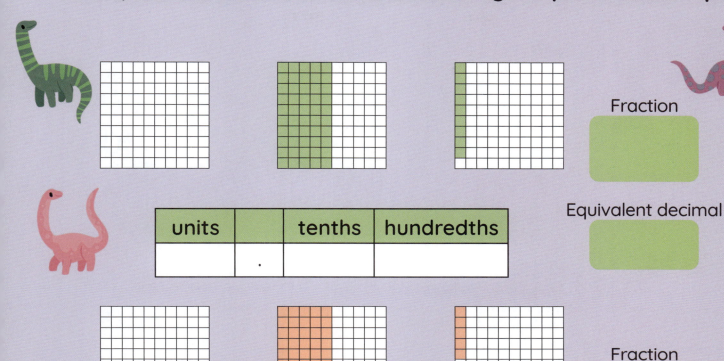

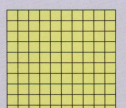
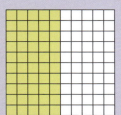
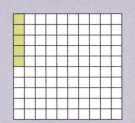

Fraction match

Match up each fraction with the correct decimal.

$\frac{7}{10}$

$\frac{7}{100}$

$\frac{33}{100}$

$\frac{9}{10}$

$\frac{9}{100}$

$\frac{3}{10}$

0.07

0.33

0.09

0.7

0.3

0.9

Equivalents

Each plate had 10 berries at the start. What fraction of fruits are left on the plate each time after the dinosaurs ate some? Write the decimal equivalents, too.

Now write the mixed fractions and their decimal equivalents.

 1 —/10 = 1.   1 —/10 = 1.

Odd one out

Each of the groups below contains equivalent numbers, except for an odd one out each time. Can you find that odd one?

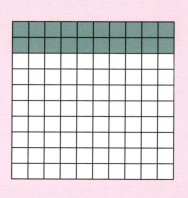 $\dfrac{20}{100}$ 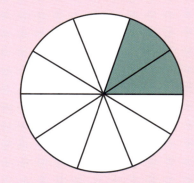 0.02 $\dfrac{2}{10}$

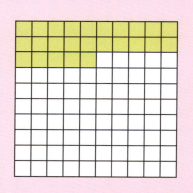 $\dfrac{25}{100}$ 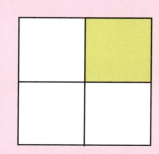 0.25 $\dfrac{1}{5}$

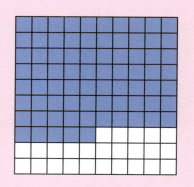 $\dfrac{75}{100}$ 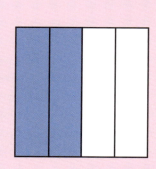 0.75 $\dfrac{3}{4}$

58

Acrocanthus adding

Help Atticus the Acrocanthus complete the calculations below, using the examples as a guide.

0.25 + 0.25 = 0.5

$\frac{1}{4} + \frac{1}{4} = \frac{1}{2}$

0.5 + 0.5 =

$\frac{1}{2} + \frac{1}{2} =$

0.35 + 0.35 =

$\frac{35}{100} + \frac{35}{100} =$

0.25 + 0.1 =

$\frac{25}{100} + \frac{10}{100} =$

0.75 + 0.25 =

$\frac{3}{4} + \frac{1}{4} =$

0.4 + 0.5 =

$\frac{4}{10} + \frac{5}{10} =$

Making 10

Give each of the dinosaurs the mail it needs to make a total of 10 each time. Draw lines to connect them.

Dividing by 10

The dinos need your help. Each container must last for 10 days. Look at how much water is in each, then work out how much they can drink each day. One has been done for you.

5 ÷ 10 =

4 ÷ 10 = 0.4

3 ÷ 10 =

1 ÷ 10 =

2 ÷ 10 =

Dividing by 100

These dinosaurs have 100 sandwiches. If only some are eaten, how do you show that as a decimal? One has been done as an example.

Number eaten	Number of sandwiches	Quantity eaten
10	100	0.1
12	100	
15	100	
20	100	
22	100	
35	100	

Rounding numbers

Round these numbers up or down to the nearest whole number. Draw lines to join the pterosaurs to the peak that matches the rounded number. Then, write the number of pterosaurs on each peak.

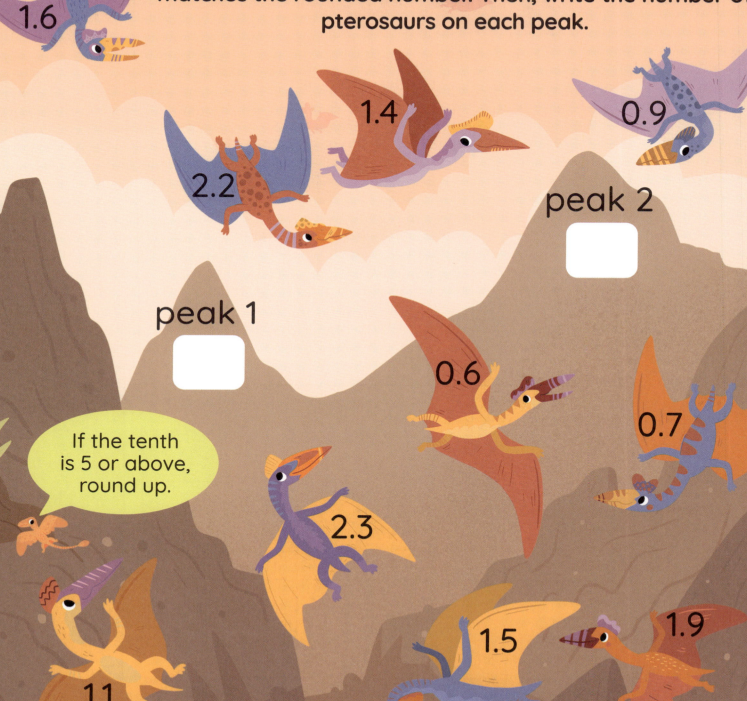

If the tenth is 5 or above, round up.

Rounding numbers

Round the numbers by each Muttaburrasaurus' head to the nearest whole number. Write the answers in the blank boxes.

Bigger or smaller?

Use the inequality symbols < and > to fill in the blank spaces between the two numbers.

less than <   > more than

10.7 ◯ 10.6

1.2 ◯ 1.3

34.25 ◯ 34.24

105.70 ◯ 105.71

Adding decimals

The two numbers below each Torosaurus should add up to the number above them. Can you fill in the missing numbers?

Tiny dinos

Each tiny dino is worth a number. Add up the dinos in each group to see which has the biggest total.

Word problems

Read each question and write your answers in the boxes.

Baby Apatosaurus is 20.25 feet long. Daddy is 70.5 feet long. What is the difference?

feet

Deinonychus sprints at 9.7 km/h. If it slows to 6.3 km/h, what is the difference?

km/h

The grown-up Maiasaura weighs 4.9 tons and the young Maiasaura weighs 2.4 tons. What is the difference?

tons

There are 60.3 gallons of water in the pool. The Maiasaura drink 10.2 gallons. How much water is left?

gallons

Dino race

These Suchomimus are having a race. Use the clues and their numbers to work out the position each finishes in.

12.44

23.72

16.8

62.68

The winner has one decimal place.

Second place has the same number of tenths and hundredths.

Third is the dinosaur with 6 tens and 8 hundredths.

Fourth is the dinosaur with 2 hundredths.

Decimals to fractions

Convert these decimals into fractions, and then put the fraction in its simplest form. The first one has been done for you.

Decimal	Equivalent fraction	Simplified fraction
0.2	$\frac{2}{10}$	$\frac{1}{5}$
0.02		
0.25		
0.6		
0.05		
0.4		
0.15		

More conversions

Do the same with these ones. You may not need to write a simplified fraction each time.

Decimal	Equivalent fraction	Simplified fraction
0.5		
0.8		
0.1		
0.9		
0.04		
0.06		
0.75		

Introducing percentages

Percent means out of a hundred, so 1% is the same as one hundredth, or 0.01. Using the example, circle the odd one out in the sections below.

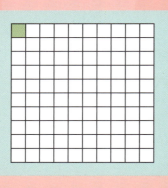 $\dfrac{1}{100}$ 1%   (0.1)   0.01

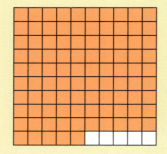 $\dfrac{95}{100}$ 95%   0.95   9.5

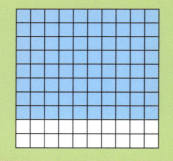 $\dfrac{80}{100}$ 8%   0.8 $\dfrac{4}{5}$

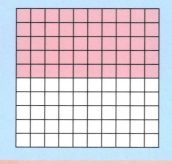 $\dfrac{50}{100}$ 50% $\dfrac{1}{2}$ 0.05

74

More percentages

Use your knowledge of percentages to help you work out which of the Archaeopteryx is the odd one out.

Converting to percentages

Follow the first example and fill in the percentages in the yellow column.

Simplest fraction	Tenths	Hundredths	Decimal	Percentage
$\frac{1}{2}$	$\frac{5}{10}$	$\frac{50}{100}$	0.5	50%
$\frac{1}{4}$		$\frac{25}{100}$	0.25	
$\frac{1}{5}$	$\frac{2}{10}$	$\frac{20}{100}$	0.2	
$\frac{1}{10}$		$\frac{10}{100}$	0.1	
$\frac{3}{5}$	$\frac{6}{10}$	$\frac{60}{100}$	0.6	
$\frac{3}{4}$		$\frac{75}{100}$	0.75	

Word problems

Read the word problems and write the answers in the boxes.

40% of the creatures on this page are club-tailed Ankylosaurus. What percentage are not?

What fraction of the creatures are long-necked sauropods? Write the fraction in its simplest form.

50% of these creatures are adults. What percentage are not?

One of these creatures is an Allosaurus. What fraction is that?

What percentage of the creatures are flying?

More word problems

Here are 20 Deinonychus and Lambeosaurus together. Read the problems carefully and then write the answers in the boxes.

Lambeosaurus have head crests. Deinonychus have feathers.

What fraction of them have red feathers?

What percentage of the dinosaurs are turquoise?

What percentage have red feathers?

What fraction of the dinosaurs are yellow?

If 55% of these dinosaurs are female, what percentage are male?

What percentage of the dinosaurs are yellow?

Work it out

Answer the questions and work out which dinosaur has the lowest number.

What is half of 2.5?

1.2

1.22

1.4

What is $\frac{2}{3}$ of 2.1?

What is one third of 3.66?

1.25

What is 75% of 2.0?

1.5

What is 50% of 2.4?

Quick calculations

See how quickly you can work out the answers to these calculations.

$\frac{22}{100}$ = ☐ % $\frac{1}{4} + \frac{5}{8}$ = ☐

$\frac{7}{10}$ = ☐ % $\frac{5}{6} + \frac{2}{6}$ = ☐ or ☐

$\frac{12}{20}$ = ☐ % $\frac{22}{100} + \frac{4}{25}$ = ☐ or ☐

$\frac{5}{50}$ = ☐ % $\frac{10}{14} - \frac{2}{7}$ = ☐ or ☐

$\frac{7}{25}$ = ☐ % $\frac{7}{9} - \frac{2}{18}$ = ☐ or ☐

Quick calculations

Here are some more speedy calculations to try.

0.2 + 0.02 = ☐   1/4 = ☐ = ☐ %

0.8 + 0.7 = ☐   1/2 = ☐ = ☐ %

3.5 + 3.16 = ☐   3/4 = ☐ = ☐ %

1.95 + 0.9 = ☐   1/5 = ☐ = ☐ %

10.4 + 1.25 = ☐   3/10 = ☐ = ☐ %

Quick calculations

Finish the calculations by writing in the missing numbers.

$\dfrac{5}{6} - \dfrac{4}{6} = \dfrac{\boxed{}}{}$ $1 - \dfrac{5}{6} = \dfrac{\boxed{}}{}$

$\dfrac{95}{100} - \dfrac{\boxed{}}{} = \dfrac{30}{100}$ $1 - \dfrac{\boxed{}}{} = \dfrac{99}{100}$

$\dfrac{\boxed{}}{} - \dfrac{4}{9} = \dfrac{3}{9}$ $\dfrac{\boxed{}}{} - \dfrac{2}{9} = \dfrac{7}{9}$

$\dfrac{1}{2} - \dfrac{1}{4} = \dfrac{\boxed{}}{}$ $1 - \dfrac{3}{4} = \dfrac{\boxed{}}{}$

$\dfrac{10}{12} - \dfrac{\boxed{}}{} = \dfrac{5}{12}$ $2 - \dfrac{\boxed{}}{} = 1\dfrac{1}{3}$

Quick calculations

Now do the same for these calculations.

$\dfrac{1}{3} + \dfrac{1}{3} = \dfrac{\boxed{}}{\boxed{}}$ $\dfrac{1}{3} + \dfrac{2}{3} = \boxed{}$

$\dfrac{46}{100} + \dfrac{\boxed{}}{\boxed{}} = \dfrac{49}{100}$ $\dfrac{13}{100} + \dfrac{\boxed{}}{\boxed{}} = 1$

$\dfrac{\boxed{}}{\boxed{}} + \dfrac{4}{6} = \dfrac{5}{6}$ $\dfrac{\boxed{}}{\boxed{}} + \dfrac{1}{10} = \dfrac{9}{10}$

$\dfrac{3}{5} + \dfrac{1}{5} = \dfrac{\boxed{}}{\boxed{}}$ $\dfrac{10}{15} + \dfrac{5}{15} = \boxed{}$

$\dfrac{4}{11} + \dfrac{\boxed{}}{\boxed{}} = 1$ $\dfrac{7}{8} + \dfrac{\boxed{}}{\boxed{}} = 1\dfrac{1}{8}$

Quick calculations

This time, finish the calculations by writing in the missing decimals.

0.8 + 0.1 = [ ]   1 + 0.3 = [ ]

0.15 + [ ] = 0.3   0.75 + [ ] = 1

[ ] + 0.2 = 0.54   [ ] + 1.3 = 2.44

0.9 + [ ] = 0.95   1.7 + [ ] = 2.75

1.4 + 0.5 = [ ]   10.14 + 0.06 = [ ]

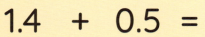

Quick calculations

Do the same for these.

0.3 − ☐ = 0.1   1 − 0.28 = ☐

0.5 − 0.25 = ☐   1 − ☐ = 0.17

☐ − 0.15 = 0.35   ☐ − 1.05 = 0.95

0.95 − ☐ = 0.82   10 − 5.7 = ☐

5.5 − 2.2 = ☐   20 − ☐ = 9.1

Whose is whose?

Work out the answers to the problems on the pink Diplodocus, and match them to the correct yellow Diplodocus.

$1 - \frac{10}{14}$

$\frac{5}{40} + \frac{5}{40}$

$3 - 1\frac{1}{5}$

50% of 14

1.8

$\frac{2}{7}$

0.25

$\frac{49}{7}$

Answers

4 Whole or half?

5 Draw the fraction

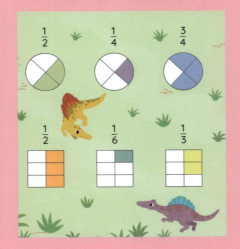

6 Find the fraction

7 How many?

8 Write the fraction

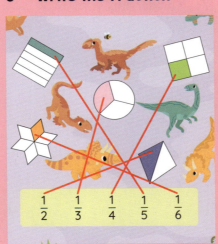

9 Draw the fraction

10 Match the fractions
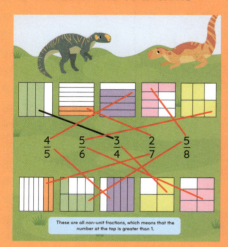

11 Word problems

12 Picture problems
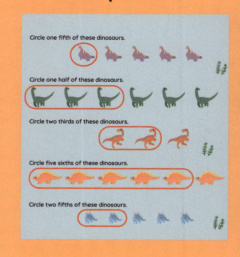

13 Word problems

14 Ordering unit fractions

15 Ordering non-unit fractions

16 Ordering non-unit fractions
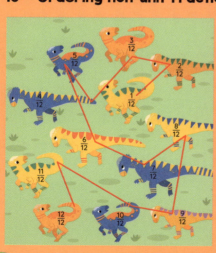

17 Shade and sort

18 Counting up
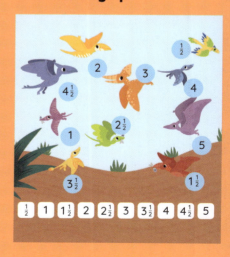

19 What's missing?

20 Equivalent fractions

21 Equivalent fractions
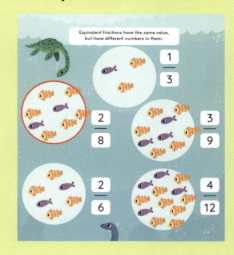

22 Fast flyers
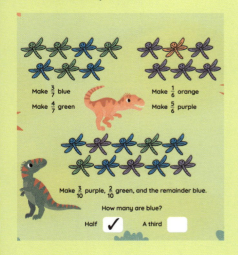

23 Equivalent fractions

24 Clock fractions
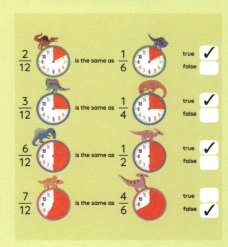

25 Equivalent fractions
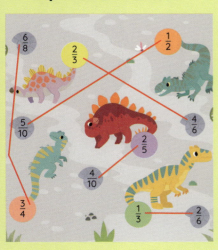

26 Equivalent fractions
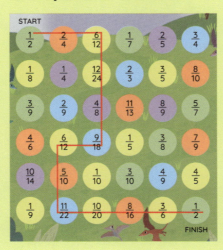

27 Simplifying fractions
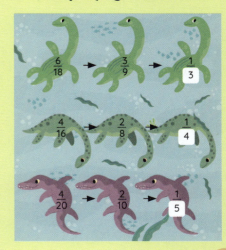

89

28 In order

29 Bigger, smaller, or the same?
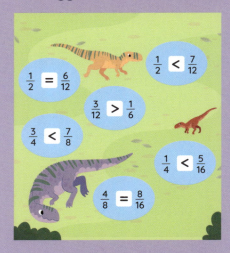

30 Adding fractions
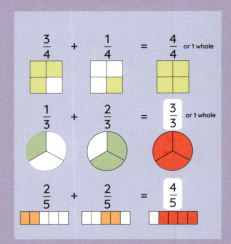

31 Adding fractions
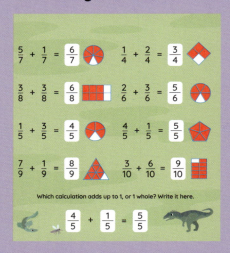

32 Word problems

33 Adding fractions
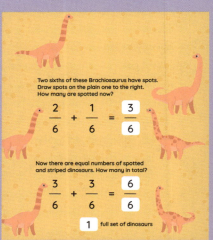

34 Adding fractions
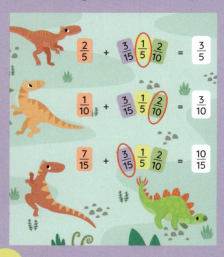

35 More adding
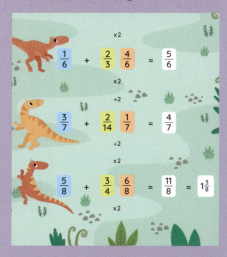

36 Subtracting fractions
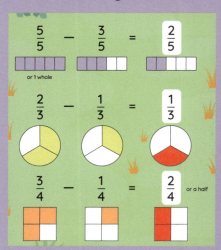

37 Subtracting fractions
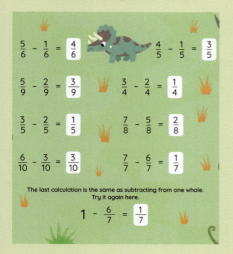

38 Word problems
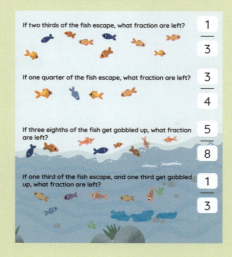

39 Subtracting fractions

40 Subtracting fractions
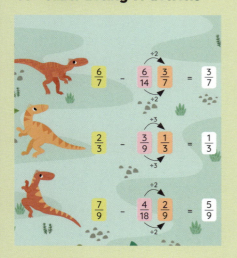

41 Convert the fractions

42 Improper fractions

43 Improper fractions

44 Understanding tenths

45 Counting in tenths
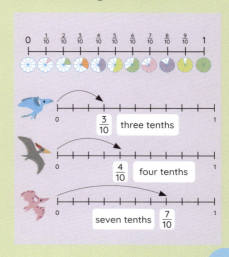

46 What's a tenth?

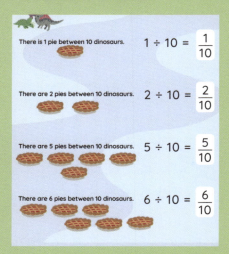

47 What's a tenth?

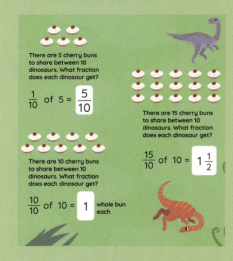

48 Writing tenths as decimals

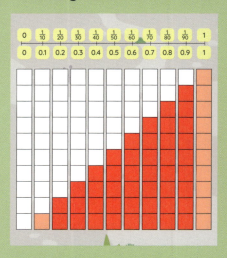

49 Odd one out

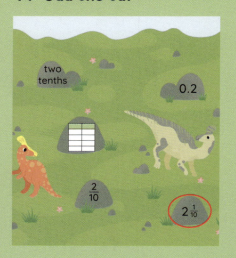

50 Ordering decimals

51 Tenths and hundredths

52 On the move

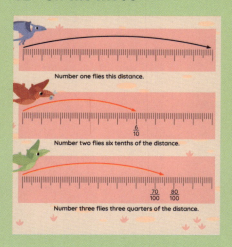

53 Place value

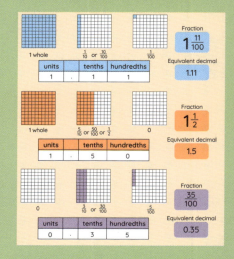

54 Fractions to decimals

55 Fractions to decimals

56 Fraction match
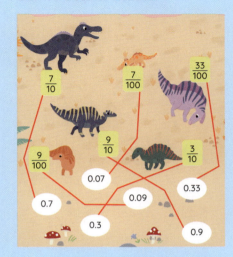

57 Equivalents
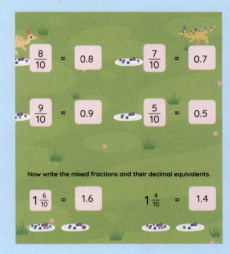

58 Odd one out
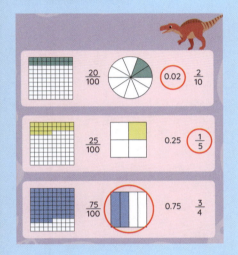

59 Acrocanthus adding

60 Making 2

61 Making 10
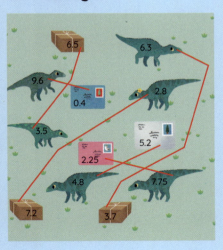

62 Dividing by 10
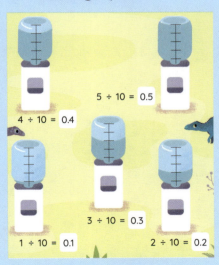

63 Dividing by 100
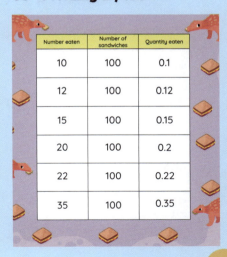

64 Rounding numbers

65 Rounding numbers

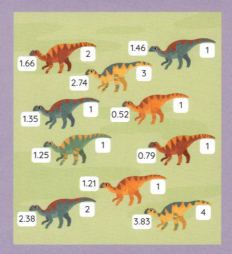

66 Ordering decimals

67 Bigger or smaller?

68 Adding decimals

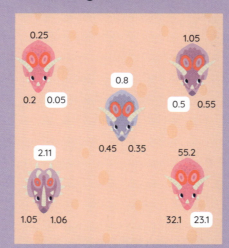

69 Tiny dinos

70 Word problems

71 Dino race

72 Decimals to fractions

Decimal	Equivalent fraction	Simplified fraction
0.2	$\frac{2}{10}$	$\frac{1}{5}$
0.02	$\frac{2}{100}$	$\frac{1}{50}$
0.25	$\frac{25}{100}$	$\frac{1}{4}$
0.6	$\frac{6}{10}$	$\frac{3}{5}$
0.05	$\frac{5}{100}$	$\frac{1}{20}$
0.4	$\frac{4}{10}$	$\frac{2}{5}$
0.15	$\frac{15}{100}$	$\frac{3}{20}$

73 More conversions

Decimal	Equivalent fraction	Simplified fraction
0.5	$\frac{5}{10}$	$\frac{1}{2}$
0.8	$\frac{8}{10}$	$\frac{4}{5}$
0.1	$\frac{1}{10}$	
0.9	$\frac{9}{10}$	
0.04	$\frac{4}{100}$	$\frac{1}{25}$
0.06	$\frac{6}{100}$	$\frac{3}{50}$
0.75	$\frac{75}{100}$	$\frac{3}{4}$

74 Introducing percentages

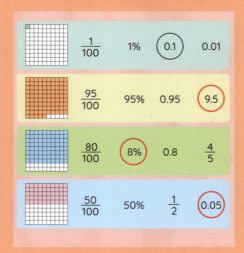

75 More percentages

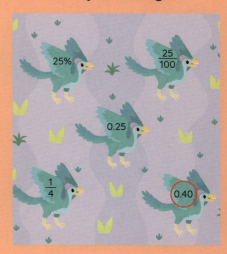

76 Converting to percentages

Simplest fraction	Tenths	Hundredths	Decimal	Percentage
$\frac{1}{2}$	$\frac{5}{10}$	$\frac{50}{100}$	0.5	50%
$\frac{1}{4}$		$\frac{25}{100}$	0.25	25%
$\frac{1}{5}$	$\frac{2}{10}$	$\frac{20}{100}$	0.2	20%
$\frac{1}{10}$		$\frac{10}{100}$	0.1	10%
$\frac{3}{5}$	$\frac{6}{10}$	$\frac{60}{100}$	0.6	60%
$\frac{3}{4}$		$\frac{75}{100}$	0.75	75%

77 Word problems

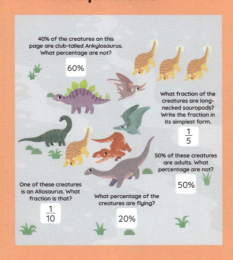

78 More word problems

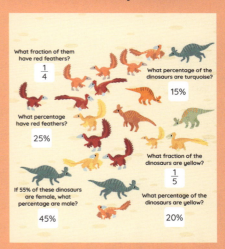

79 Work it out

80 Quick calculations

$\frac{22}{100}$ = 22% $\frac{1}{4} + \frac{5}{8} = \frac{7}{8}$

$\frac{7}{10}$ = 70% $\frac{5}{6} + \frac{2}{6} = \frac{7}{6}$ or $1\frac{1}{6}$

$\frac{12}{20}$ = 60% $\frac{22}{100} + \frac{4}{25} = \frac{38}{100}$ or $\frac{19}{50}$

$\frac{5}{50}$ = 10% $\frac{10}{14} - \frac{2}{7} = \frac{6}{14}$ or $\frac{3}{7}$

$\frac{7}{25}$ = 28% $\frac{7}{9} - \frac{2}{18} = \frac{12}{18}$ or $\frac{1}{3}$

81 Quick calculations

0.2 + 0.02 = 0.22 $\frac{1}{4}$ = 0.25 = 25%

0.8 + 0.7 = 1.5 $\frac{1}{2}$ = 0.5 = 50%

3.5 + 3.16 = 6.66 $\frac{3}{4}$ = 0.75 = 75%

1.95 + 0.9 = 2.85 $\frac{1}{5}$ = 0.2 = 20%

10.4 + 1.25 = 11.65 $\frac{3}{10}$ = 0.3 = 30%

82 Quick calculations

$\frac{5}{6} - \frac{4}{6} = \frac{1}{6}$ $\quad$ $1 - \frac{5}{6} = \frac{1}{6}$

$\frac{95}{100} - \frac{65}{100} = \frac{30}{100}$ $\quad$ $1 - \frac{1}{100} = \frac{99}{100}$

$\frac{7}{9} - \frac{4}{9} = \frac{3}{9}$ $\quad$ $1 - \frac{2}{9} = \frac{7}{9}$

$\frac{1}{2} - \frac{1}{4} = \frac{1}{4}$ $\quad$ $1 - \frac{3}{4} = \frac{1}{4}$

$\frac{10}{12} - \frac{5}{12} = \frac{5}{12}$ $\quad$ $2 - \frac{2}{3} = 1\frac{1}{3}$

83 Quick calculations

$\frac{1}{3} + \frac{1}{3} = \frac{2}{3}$ $\quad$ $\frac{1}{3} + \frac{2}{3} = 1$

$\frac{46}{100} + \frac{3}{100} = \frac{49}{100}$ $\quad$ $\frac{13}{100} + \frac{87}{100} = 1$

$\frac{1}{6} + \frac{4}{6} = \frac{5}{6}$ $\quad$ $\frac{8}{10} + \frac{1}{10} = \frac{9}{10}$

$\frac{3}{5} + \frac{1}{5} = \frac{4}{5}$ $\quad$ $\frac{10}{15} + \frac{5}{15} = 1$

$\frac{4}{11} + \frac{7}{11} = 1$ $\quad$ $\frac{7}{8} + \frac{2}{8} = 1\frac{1}{8}$

84 Quick calculations

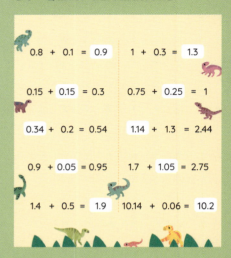

$0.8 + 0.1 = 0.9$ $\quad$ $1 + 0.3 = 1.3$

$0.15 + 0.15 = 0.3$ $\quad$ $0.75 + 0.25 = 1$

$0.34 + 0.2 = 0.54$ $\quad$ $1.14 + 1.3 = 2.44$

$0.9 + 0.05 = 0.95$ $\quad$ $1.7 + 1.05 = 2.75$

$1.4 + 0.5 = 1.9$ $\quad$ $10.14 + 0.06 = 10.2$

85 Quick calculations

$0.3 - 0.2 = 0.1$ $\quad$ $1 - 0.28 = 0.72$

$0.5 - 0.25 = 0.25$ $\quad$ $1 - 0.83 = 0.17$

$0.5 - 0.15 = 0.35$ $\quad$ $2 - 1.05 = 0.95$

$0.95 - 0.13 = 0.82$ $\quad$ $10 - 5.7 = 4.3$

$5.5 - 2.2 = 3.3$ $\quad$ $20 - 10.9 = 9.1$

86 Whose is whose?

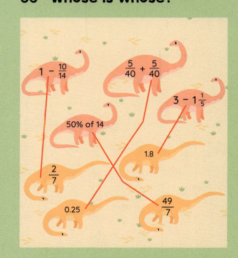

$1 - \frac{10}{14}$ $\quad$ $\frac{5}{40} + \frac{5}{40}$

$3 - 1\frac{1}{5}$

50% of 14

1.8

$\frac{2}{7}$

0.25 $\quad$ $\frac{49}{7}$